VIRTUAL WORKPLACE BLUEPRINT

MARI BLAZE

COPYRIGHT

Copyright © 2021 by MARI BLAZE: All rights reserved. This book or any portion thereof may not be reproduced or used in any manner whatsoever without the express written permission of the author except for the use of brief quotations in a book review.

TABLE OF CONTENTS

- **INTRODUCTION** 4
- **CHAPTER 1** 5
  - ADVANTAGES OF REMOTE WORKING 5
    - *Employee engagement* 5
    - *Productivity rises* 6
    - *Meetings with a Purpose* 6
- **CHAPTER 2** 7
  - WORKPLACE VIRTUAL REALITY 7
    - *Second-screen experience* 7
    - *Productivity* 8
- **CHAPTER 3** 10
  - WORKING FROM A DISTANCE 10
    - *Freelance* 11
    - *Fully remote work* 12
    - *Flexible work* 13
- **CHAPTER 4** 16
  - VIRTUAL WORKPLACE PLATFORMS 16
    - *Communication tools* 16
    - *Project and team collaboration tools* 17
    - *Tools for Organization* 17
    - *Tools for compliance* 18
    - *Tools for Organization* 18
    - *Tools for compliance* 18
    - *Recruitment tools include* 19
    - *Finance* 20
    - *Tools for virtual team games* 20
- **CHAPTER 5** 21
  - REMOTE WORKING CULTURE 21
    - *Purpose* 22
    - *Adaptability* 23
    - *Trust* 24

CHAPTER 6 ....**26**

  VIRTUAL WELLBEING IDEAS 26
    Gift Cards for a Healthy Lifestyle: 27
    Virtual Lunch and Learns 28
    Virtual Party 29
    Kindness Quest 30
    Virtual Games 31

CHAPTER 7 ....**32**

  VIRTUAL WORK MODELS 32
    Affiliate marketing 33
    Upskilling 33
    Sponsorship 34
    Ecommerce: 35
    Influencer marketing 36
    Subscription: 36

INTRODUCTION

For a long time, the corporate world has been evolving, pushed on by advances in computers and other technology that have allowed us to spread out geographically and get work done from almost anywhere. More and more firms are allowing employees to spend their days working from a non-traditional work environment, such as a remote office, a home office, or even a neighbourhood coffee shop. For workers who are dissatisfied with traditional career prospects, a virtual team is an increasing trend. These seasoned professionals are freelancers, part-timers, and side hustlers who apply their local knowledge in a worldwide setting. Flexibility in the workplace is a hot topic in the future of employment. Is this tendency, however, economically justified, or is it simply a result of our changing workforce's need for modern convenience? The fact remains that in today's business world, job flexibility is the standard.

This book aims to create the fundamental blueprint for the virtual workplace.

CHAPTER 1
ADVANTAGES OF REMOTE WORKING

Not only is it crucial to be able to view your co-worker's work, but it's also crucial to be able to interact with and change it in real-time. Recently, there has been a lot of talk about remote employment in the headlines. When a company requires flexible working hours, virtual offices allow employees to work whenever and from wherever they want. Workplace experts are disputing the nature of the necessity for traditional physical workplaces in a world packed with collaboration tools, communication gadgets, connection apps, and mobile digital computers. Employers must be acquainted and skilled with online collaborative technologies, grasp the workplace psychology of space and distance, and know-how to cultivate certain team dynamics in order to achieve success in virtual teams.

Employee engagement: This is enhanced by the presence of a virtual team. When employees are happy with their working conditions, they are more likely to be active. In virtual teams, higher productivity leads to improved performance. Some employees prefer to work from home because it allows them to have a more flexible schedule, spend more time with their families, work while travelling, and run errands or do chores during their breaks.

Productivity rises: Being a part of a virtual team is such a powerful incentive that it allows people to work more efficiently in a virtual environment. Setting clear expectations and criteria for job performance and productivity makes it easier for virtual teams to track and assess their results. When you decide to form a virtual team, you are no longer limited to the abilities and abilities accessible within your organization or local community; instead, you may tap into a global pool of talent with a few mouse clicks. Virtual workplace diversity boosts productivity to new heights. Due to the combined efforts of time zone differences among employees around the world, a firm can operate 24 hours a day, seven days a week.

Meetings with a Purpose: Keeping accurate time records and reporting is simple with a virtual workplace. Virtual meetings, on the other hand, necessitate preparation and planning. Employees who work remotely can use any technology they want, and they're in charge of upgrading it when it's convenient for them. Remote meetings and collaborative project management software can help virtual teams save time.

CHAPTER 2

WORKPLACE VIRTUAL REALITY

Virtual reality is a technique that uses computer-generated 3D environments to replace physical reality. Although virtual reality, which has been hailed as the next big thing in technology, has yet to catch on as a consumer product, companies are seeing it as a more efficient and effective tool for on-the-job training. Working online and interacting with digital technologies both inside and beyond the office walls has become a need and the usual for the majority of organizations. Long-term video interactions may create weariness, leaving us exhausted. Virtual reality (VR) appears to be the solution to being visually present with people without needing to be on camera. Virtual reality is transforming the way we learn, complete activities, and interact with the world, and it's not just for fun. While millennials may have been the first to embrace virtual reality, human productivity has been waiting for a tool like VR for far longer than the gaming industry.

Second-screen experience: One of the most basic goals of technology, in general, is to protect people from harm. Virtual reality is attempting to fulfil that promise in a novel way. Virtual reality is transforming the way we both play and work. As a catalyst for better collaboration, virtual reality can be used. You may enter a collaborative and immersive virtual environment as soon as you put on the headset and noise-cancelling headphones. Virtual reality training isn't appropriate in every workplace. Some tactile skills, for example, are better learned through hands-on practice. The technology, on the other hand, is particularly useful for preparing people for the novel or emergency scenarios. Virtual reality has already had an impact on training. Employers can use virtual reality to imitate real-life scenarios, exposing staff to circumstances like resolving client complaints, dissatisfaction, and how to turn an upset client into a pleased one. These virtual reality systems can provide medical professionals with the most up-to-date training without the need for less realistic simulations or even human testing. Virtual reality can link employees and customers beyond physical borders in the workplace.

Productivity: This generation values a high level of flexibility, mobility, and, in general, a strong work-life balance. Virtual reality increases cognition and memorability. Interacting with 3D models rather than analyzing 2D sketches makes it easier to study subjects like anatomy and cosmology. Companies may now give continuous expert knowledge training across their ranks using virtual reality. It assists them in establishing a consistent, company-wide framework based on ongoing learning. In VR, management can experiment with various work and production processes without incurring the high costs that real-world experimentation requires. VR's immersive environment allows for a more permanent imprint on memory and caters to a different learning style that helps to reinforce knowledge and increase recall. VR allows employees from various departments or corporate locations to collaborate virtually over long distances.

CHAPTER 3
WORKING FROM A DISTANCE

With the aid of modern technology, it is now feasible to work in unusual ways, and the employment market has changed substantially as a result. Many businesses are seeing the benefits of remote work, and the number of flexible jobs may continue to rise. Working from home or telecommuting are terms used to describe work done outside of a regular office setting. How we work, study, play, spend our leisure time, interact, and obtain information has altered dramatically since the Internet's inception a few decades ago. Remote working, or working entirely outside of your company's office, is a completely different experience. It necessitates a unique set of talents, resources, and abilities. It necessitates a can-do attitude and ridiculous time management abilities. Because you don't get to see your colleagues on a daily basis, it also necessitates proactive communication and an almost hyperfocus on what's going on with them. Video conferencing, texting, cell phones, and email are all options today. We can save our work on the cloud and share it with our coworkers and superiors. Employees can successfully complete projects and daily activities without having to commute to an office every day, according to the concept of remote work. For years, the remote work revolution has been rumbling across industries, and it is far from over. Flexible working is a given, but remote working is gaining popularity. Remote working necessitates the creation of your own work environment, which has obvious advantages because you can design your workplace to suit your needs. On the same hand, unless you build it yourself, you don't have the safety of an office, cubicle, or desk to retreat to when you need to hunker down. Performance management has altered dramatically as a result of remote employment. People feel empowered to work in a style that suits them and the organization, thus remote workers are less anxious, and there is less tension in the office and workplace. Organizations will increasingly place a premium on results rather than hours spent, necessitating the use of tools and apps to oversee remote employee performance. Remote workers are less expensive, and supporting diverse ways of working allows businesses to save money on rent and property. Now, let's look at how we may categorize remote work.

Freelance: Freelancing is here to stay today, because of the tremendous workforce migration to the gig economy. The rise of freelance platforms such as TaskRabbit, Upwork, Fiverr, Toptal, and others has gained widespread acceptance in a number of countries. This refers to projects or work done by independent contractors. A freelance job is one in which an individual work for himself or herself rather than for a company. Because of this flexibility, it's common for freelancers to work on many projects for different clients at the same time, while certain freelancing contracts may prevent the worker from taking on further work until the project is completed. While freelancers work for firms and organizations on a contract basis, they are ultimately self-employed. Freelancing began as a fad, a poor man's alternative to gruelling 9-to-5 office jobs. Not everyone is suited to freelancing. As a freelancer, those who prefer a lot of handholding along the way throughout project completion may feel alienated. If you work best in a group, you may find it difficult to succeed if you spend a lot of time working alone. Work as a freelancer isn't always predictable, which is a major distinction from typical employment. Getting enough customers to pay the bills can be difficult as well. A freelancer is a self-employed entrepreneur who works on side projects and on a smaller scale. Many freelancers work part-time or full-time in addition to their regular jobs. Some freelancers hope to turn their side gig into a full-time gig. Digital marketing, customer support, coding, graphics design, social media management, consulting, writing, and editing are just a few of the fields where freelance work is most common.

Fully remote work: When it comes to fully remote work, finding the proper personnel and assisting them in becoming a part of the firm is critical. Fully remote businesses are selective in their hiring practices. They also enjoy being inventive when it comes to reinforcing business culture and employee bonds. Remote workers should be self-starters who are highly driven and accountable. Organizations often equip employees with everything they need to fulfil their tasks. In a remote work setting, when employees must provide all they need to execute their jobs, the opposite may be true. You will not be required to go to an office if you operate completely remotely. This often means that, based on the regulations and obligations of the organization, you can work in your own home, in a co-working place, or even at the beach if you want to. Fully remote employees work full-time for a company with a regular office from their remote locations. They have a clear wage rate or income, and the occupations are typically career-oriented with advancement opportunities. I once had a buddy who was offered a remote job in Germany but couldn't take it since he wasn't in the country at the time, so he opted for fully remote employment in the country he was in but was turned down due to tax rules and company duties. When an employee utilizes the same site for both professional and personal matters, the border between the two can get blurred. In what is sometimes referred to as a remote work agreement, organizations should put the fundamental terms of a remote work arrangement in writing.

Flexible work: Workplace flexibility refers to an organization's readiness and ability to adapt to change, particularly in terms of how and when work is completed. Flexible working is a fantastic alternative to the typical office paradigm of work. Flexible employees keep the company's goals in mind and work to attain them, adjusting their efforts to the current purpose. Flexible working is often known as working from home or creating your own work hours. Although a nine-to-five job with a set schedule provides more predictability and stability, many people choose flexible work options that allow them to better combine their professional and personal lives. This type of model was once the domain of freelancers, but since the epidemic hit and the world fell apart, more and more businesses throughout the world are embracing it to ensure that their businesses stay alive. The flexibility to work flexibly is one of the most essential and effective perks you may receive from your business. Flexibility in the workplace is a method for adapting to changing conditions and expectations. Employee retention and engagement are frequently aided by workplace flexibility. Media, business, sports, education, administration, hospitality, science, and technology all benefit from flexible work. These days, flexible jobs are becoming more common. Organizations sometimes give flexibility in terms of scheduling, location, or both. Some flexible employment work in the opposite direction, allowing workers to work from home most of the time yet commute to the office once a week for in-person meetings. Employees in this situation are normally required to live in the city where the office is located. Companies are recognizing that providing employees with more work-life balance helps to keep them happy, and happy employees are more productive employees. Sales and marketing, software development, virtual assistant, customer service, project management, speech-language pathologist, computer and IT, accounting and finance, education and training, data scientist, interior designer, personal trainer, dog walker, online tutor, and a variety of other fields frequently prefer flexible jobs.

CHAPTER 4

VIRTUAL WORKPLACE PLATFORMS

For remote teams who are unable to meet in person on a daily basis, virtual workspaces can serve as a collaborative center. While remote teams can communicate via internal communications software or video conferencing software, virtual workplaces offer structure and a framework for engagement that would otherwise be lacking. Virtual work software can help remote teams succeed by allowing in-house and off-site workers to collaborate on projects regardless of their geographical location. The finest virtual work software is a solution that successfully establishes a shared online workplace that remote employees may utilize to do tasks in a virtual setting. Remote collaboration tools are software programs that aid virtual teams in obtaining and sharing information in the most efficient manner possible. A competent virtual work program can tenfold boost overall team efficiency while also streamlining digital communication on a project.

Communication tools: In virtual teams, communication between team members, clients, and suppliers is critical for enhancing productivity and optimizing time management. The communication platform should include video calling, instant messaging, file sharing and storage, a presentation screen, and other real-time tools to improve communication in a virtual area.

Skype, Zoom, Slack, Google Meet, Microsoft Teams, and Yammer are just a few of the most popular collaboration technologies.

Project and team collaboration tools: The quickest method to boost productivity is to reduce workplace distractions. It's a good idea to use tools to help organize video meetings, training, and webinars so that staff can get together. Virtual teams must work together on a single document. Project and team collaboration can be done in real-time in an online drive – also known as cloud storage – so that everyone has access to the same file. Google Drive, OneDrive, Google Docs, Canva, Dropbox, Asana, GitHub, TeamViewer, and a variety of additional apps are all worth considering. Individuals and teams must work together and plan carefully to get a large project through to completion.

Tools for Organization: The same ideas that apply to physical environments may be applied to virtual workplaces. Virtual events are becoming increasingly popular since they have shown to be more entertaining, interactive, cost-effective, accessible, and managed than live events. Every company need to have its own set of tools. Choosing the correct tools for virtual event planning might help you be more creative and productive. In a virtual office, a work calendar is essential, and it should have functions like calendar management, time management, social media management, and note-taking. Calendly, Hubstaff, HootSuite, and Evernote are some of the most popular tools in this category.

Tools for compliance: There is a digital tool for anything these days, including contract signings if you can't be in the same room at the same time to sign those important papers. Make sure the virtual meeting platform you chose has features that will allow you to meet future needs. This should include features such as password management, E-Signature, security, and legal considerations. DocuSign, HelloSign, LastPass, and a few others are some of the most popular solutions in this category.

Tools for Organization: The same ideas that apply to physical environments may be applied to virtual workplaces. Virtual events are becoming increasingly popular since they have shown to be more entertaining, interactive, cost-effective, accessible, and managed than live events. Every company need to have its own set of tools. Choosing the correct tools for virtual event planning might help you be more creative and productive. In a virtual office, a work calendar is essential, and it should have functions like calendar management, time management, social media management, and note-taking. Calendly, Hubstaff, HootSuite, and Evernote are some of the most popular tools in this category.

Tools for compliance: There is a digital tool for anything these days, including contract signings if you can't be in the same room at the same time to sign those important papers. Make sure the virtual meeting platform you chose has features that will allow you to meet future needs. This should include features such as password management, E-Signature, security, and legal considerations. DocuSign, HelloSign, LastPass, and a few others are some of the most popular solutions in this category.

Recruitment tools include: It's no secret that the longer a job search takes, the more money it costs. However, knowing how to recruit staffs online without using complex and expensive tools isn't always straightforward. Fortunately, the high expenses associated with long-term vacancies can be avoided by improving the speed and cost-effectiveness of hiring. The internet is democratizing the recruitment process; resources that were once only available through pricey recruitment agencies are now widely available at a minimal cost, and in some cases, for free. Recruiters must maintain track of and consider applicant experience, employee recommendations, candidate skills, employee references, and other candidate information while recruiting, screening, interviewing, and employing candidates. They also require a method of distilling this data into a final recruiting choice. Virtual workspaces make it simple to find, hire, train, and retain people from all around the world. Whether it's evaluating candidate profiles or locating contact information for potential clients, every member of the recruitment industry understands the value of efficiency in the recruiting process. Using tools that automate answers, compile data profiles, and give a platform for the entire process, technology and digital systems are the most effective approach to optimize your recruiting strategy and improve your candidate's experience. TalentLMS, Checkr, Workable, HackerRank, BambooHR, and a few more are some of the best platforms for managing talent in virtual workplaces.

Finance: These tools can assist with budgeting, tracking, billing, payments, receipt management, and expense management. Expensify, Float, QuickBooks, LivePlan, Xero, and Scoro are some of the programs to employ.

Tools for virtual team games: Virtual team games improve communication and trust. QuizBreaker, Water Cooler Trivia, Prelude, and VirtuWall are some of the tools that can be used to construct virtual team games.

CHAPTER 5
REMOTE WORKING CULTURE

Simply said, culture is the way things are done. Having a set of settings can help you control the direction that remote working goes. Long-term remote work may be desired by many employees since, as travel times have decreased, so have opportunities for important relationship-building at work. Instead of prescribing a one-size-fits-all manner of working, technology developed by diverse teams may result in more adaptable solutions to let people accomplish their best job in their own way. Organizations require more than just the ability to articulate their culture. They must understand the culture's drivers, such as values, beliefs, traditions, structures, unwritten norms, behaviours, and the recurring events that shape the employee experience and shape the culture. An excellent remote firm should feel similar to one with a physical location. Finally, more inclusive solutions can help individuals collaborate without needing to be in the same physical area or working at the same time, making remote workers feel just as connected to the organization and its mission as those who share a physical space onsite. A fantastic strategy to introduce a healthy virtual workplace is to create a remote work culture deck and share it on the web for others to see. During a period of disruption, it's a good idea to remind employees of the company's history, founding ideas, stories, and commitments that have defined its culture and identity. Building up these basic characteristics of culture may remind employees of the company's strengths while also assisting them in through difficult times.

Employee happiness, engagement, retention, and recruitment are all directly influenced by company culture. It can, however, be used as a competitive advantage. At all levels, culture has an impact on business decisions. To establish a relationship between a company and its employees, more is required. Mindfulness, intention, and rethinking are required. When a company's basic principles are upheld, its culture transforms employees into advocates, improves their well-being, and ensures that top talent is retained. When it comes to organizing projects and pulling the team together into a cohesive one, a virtual workforce necessitates higher leadership abilities. Employers must create a virtual environment in which team members feel connected and safe in order to maintain remote workplace culture. Employees must believe that their entire team is working together to stay productive and that their input is valued. The ideas outlined below should be the foundation of remote working culture.

Purpose: The simple definition of remote work is that it is done for a specific reason; this is what gives virtual labour its significance. Positive workplace values should be the focus of business philosophy. In the sense of thinking about the purpose and values of what should be done every day, mindfulness is a virtue that connects with purpose. Retention rates improve when there is a sense of purpose. Organizations having a strong purpose attract Gen Z and Millennials. Profit cannot be classed as a goal, but it can be classified as a result. Offering genuine benefit to others is what purpose entails. Purpose refers to the direction in which a company wishes to travel, whereas values serve as a road map for getting there. Purpose is a goal; getting there is a trip, and all journeys entail risk, a change of scenery, and the prospect of failure. These are the barriers that most people and organizations face when it comes to transforming their mission. The virtual workplace's culture must have a defined purpose, which should be communicated to all remote workers. Purpose is an important component of a strong organizational culture. Employees that are proud of what they do and who enjoy working for the company become natural brand boosters. The employee value proposition must be connected with purpose.

Adaptability: Adaptability is one of the most important aspects of a company's strategy. In good times, culture is what makes firms terrific places to work, and in bad times, it's what keeps them together. Adaptability is the foundation of the remote work culture. Business executives understand how critical it is to be versatile in order to weather market swings and successfully handle operational issues. Organizations that are flexible have a better chance of surviving than those that are slow to pivot when change is required. People that aren't adaptable are stubborn and set in their ways. Leaders may foster a culture of adaptability by displaying their own flexibility and adaptability. While a results-oriented culture should promote competitiveness, personal initiative, and achievement, agility and flexibility are two crucial aspects for a business to be stable and grow in any adverse situation. Adaptability would assist remote organizations in realizing and maintaining their full potential independent of internal and external changes.

Trust: The value of trust inside a firm cannot be overstated. Building and maintaining strong relationships is critical not just for the success of a business, but also for its survival. Over time, trust is earned and solid relationships are formed. A trust-based culture fosters a favourable work atmosphere and motivates employees, resulting in higher production. Employee turnover can be reduced by fostering a culture of trust because trusting employees are more likely to be loyal to their employers. Transparency in the virtual workplace would help to foster strong friendships and connections. Building trust requires open, honest, and straightforward communication. Capability, contracts, and communication are the foundations of trust. Capability trust enables employees in a virtual workplace to make decisions while supervisors are confident that their opinion is valuable. When there is consistency in terms of maintaining commitments and managing expectations, trust-based on contract develops. Sharing information, delivering constructive comments, and speaking with purpose about individuals are all ways to build communication trust.

CHAPTER 6

VIRTUAL WELLBEING IDEAS

There is compelling evidence that employment, health, and well-being are inextricably intertwined and must be handled as a whole. Workers' well-being is jeopardized not just by changes in the workplace and workplace dangers, but also by the interaction of work and nonwork elements. The nature of work, the workforce, and the workplace are rapidly changing in significant ways. In the field of workplace safety and health, the term "well-being" is frequently employed. Workplace well-being takes into account both physical and mental health while on the job. Physical well-being in the workplace is influenced by factors such as room temperature, ergonomics, and activity level. Stress, depression, and anxiety are all examples of mental health issues. Mental health concerns can sometimes contribute to physical ailments and vice versa. Workplace wellness programs are realistic goals for improving an employee's mental and physical health so they can function at their best. The stigma surrounding the mental disease has portrayed persons suffering from mental illness as irrational, weak, or even insane.

The beauty of wellness is that it can be pursued from any location on the planet. The concept of virtual wellbeing is becoming a reality. The path to wellbeing can still be followed without difficulty. Online yoga courses, online nutritionists, free YouTube exercises, gift vouchers, and other virtual wellness services have paved the way. Employee wellness can be harmed by remote work because of loneliness or unforeseen impediments to working. Isolation is a problem for remote employees, so wellness initiatives should encourage them to adopt healthy practices. Wellness initiatives are designed to reduce absence and liability while also improving health and happiness in the virtual workplace. Virtual employee wellness program ideas are innovative ways to promote remote workers' mental, social, and physical health. Despite shifting to an entirely virtual work from home environment, it's critical that corporate health efforts continue. Instead, because employees are more susceptible both physically and mentally, efforts should be quadrupled. Employees who are too comfortable and no longer follow their fitness and self-affirmation goals may get out of shape as a result of remote working. While many firms currently have sophisticated employee health programs, many of them are unlikely to be designed to accommodate a remote workforce. Virtual employee wellness program ideas are innovative ways to promote remote workers' mental, social, and physical health.

Gift Cards for a Healthy Lifestyle: This incentive focuses on creating a healthy hub that allows remote teams to easily access health services at any time. This is a fantastic approach for remote employees to take care of themselves. There are a number of strategies to ensure that, even though the team is virtual, the connection and link between members remain intact. Remote workers can spend between $50 and $100 per month on services like fitness classes, healthy snack boxes, gym memberships, meditation classes, cooking classes, house cleaning, music lessons, or salons. Employees submit receipts for reimbursement and are reimbursed for their expenses. Since we work from home, we should have had a better work-life balance, right? Theoretically, sure. The truth, however, is rather different. Not everyone has the resources, connections, or openness to reach out to others on their own. This is quite common in people who are suffering from mental illness and are willing to suffer in quiet. Having remote employees attend private one-on-one meetings is a good way to alleviate their fears and concerns. Hearing some inspirational and motivational speeches is always a good way to lift your spirits, increase your morale, and inspire you.

Virtual Lunch and Learns: A lunch and learn is a laid-back presentation or training session for employees. Styles and styles vary, but it usually consists of a single topic covered over the course of a lunch hour. Employers can choose from a variety of topics ranging from personal financial wellness to stress management strategies, all of which can be taught by local experts or even employees. Virtual lunch and learns can be developed using platforms like Zoom, where remote workers can take a break and share something fascinating that is going on in their lives. In virtual lunch and learn events, icebreaker questions could be used. Icebreaker questions are basic inquiries that help team members learn more about one another. For example, you can begin a remote conference by asking each participant to give their name, role, favourite colour, pet's name, and favourite breakfast food. Lunch and learn events might be recorded and added to the healthy wellbeing hub. This might help to promote a virtual office health culture, with virtual happy hours and interesting lunch and learn events. When team members are engaged, informed, and connected, remote working can be a lot of fun.

Virtual Party: Just because we're working remotely doesn't mean we can't celebrate birthdays and anniversaries and other noteworthy events in our lives. Before you can arrange an awesome virtual party that your visitors will never forget, there are a few things you need to keep in mind. With a virtual party, you can send out invitations, have a cake delivered, sing happy birthday, and show your team members the love they deserve. When you watch a movie together, but separately, physical distance creates room for digital intimacy. To hold the virtual party, find a virtual space. Netflix Party makes synchronization simple for movie buffs, and it even includes a group chat platform for those pesky audience remarks that add to the group movie-watching experience. Don't forget to bring some popcorn. Being apart doesn't have to ruin the party; have a virtual party that allows all team members to interact even if they can't physically meet. There is no limit to the types of events you may host electronically, from birthday celebrations to workplace milestone events.

Kindness Quest: Team-building events are critical because your employees need a way to relieve job-related stress while also getting to know their co-workers so they can work together more effectively. Kindness quest is a mission to conduct one random act of kindness every day, no matter how modest it is. The purpose of the kindness quest is to motivate team members to spread happiness, cheer, and warmth to others. A kindness quest could also be a series of enjoyable activities aimed to improve co-workers days. The purpose of this event is to teach individuals new techniques to make other people smile. If you have some free time, see if someone needs assistance with something. It's difficult to tell when a co-worker is having trouble in a virtual setting, but they'll appreciate the assistance. Send a little gift card to a local coffee shop to brighten someone's day and boost their energy levels. These activities will lift people's spirits and encourage them to volunteer for a worthwhile cause. Kindness not only makes people feel good, but it also reminds you of the power of your actions. Taking a few minutes out of your hectic day to help someone else can have a long-term impact on them. Genuine praises are remembered for a long time, and favours can keep someone afloat in a difficult situation.

Virtual Games: Virtual games are used at work to have fun, relax, and improve teamwork. Every manager is concerned about the bonds that exist among his or her employees. They should keep everyone participating in team procedures at all times, encouraging them to be more than just co-workers. Pixel art, guess the emoji, virtual campfires, virtual dance parties, and typing speed are just a few examples of inventive virtual games. Experienced team leaders understand the need of providing positive, playful support to one another. Informal team-building exercises and games are an effective approach to boost team spirit and strengthen employee bonds. Virtual games for large groups are internet games meant for groups of ten or more people to play together. There's a game for everyone online, whether it's trivia, bingo, word games, or card games. Simultaneous participation features, such as trivia or quizzes, are common in these games.

CHAPTER 7

VIRTUAL WORK MODELS

A business model explains how a company generates value and makes money, as well as how it plans to achieve its vision and goal. All of the company's policies and procedures can be considered part of the company's business model. Companies will need to beef up their present tactics, be flexible, and put their employees' safety and well-being first in order to successfully move into this next phase of work. It is critical for firms to incorporate a remote worker-friendly culture into their strategy. The pandemic has exacerbated current trends like as remote work, e-commerce, and automation, with up to 25% more employees than originally expected needing to change jobs. Organizations would naturally tend toward company models that are low on capital expenditures and high on revenues as their business acumen grows. Learning about the models ahead of time will help you make more money in the long run. The business model includes all of the business processes and policies that a company adopts and follows. There hasn't been a compelling commercial case for moving to a virtual labour environment until now. Yes, there were always financial savings to be gained, but they were frequently overshadowed by inefficiencies in the workforce. It is a crucial aspect of the organization, as it is not just about how the company produces money, but also about how it leverages key business partnerships and respects its people. More and more firms are going entirely remote these days, and they're thriving as a result. Today, more than ever, knowing how to construct a good virtual team is critical. Those who embrace the Virtual Workforce Model will be better equipped to deal with uncertainty.

Affiliate marketing: There are numerous advantages to using an affiliate marketing model. For one thing, if you follow the SEO path with your website, it's a rather passive approach. Rather than using affiliate networks, the great majority of affiliate offers originate directly from the company. Selling goods and services for brands in exchange for a fee has a long history. When done correctly, affiliate marketing may be ethical, tremendously beneficial to the end-user, and a win-win situation for both the firm that generated the offer and the affiliate who promotes it. Building a medium to a large website that is strategically monetized by specialized affiliate offers is one form of Affiliate Marketing.

Upskilling: The typical way of assembling a team of highly specialized professional's results in workers learning skills they rarely use or performing tasks that aren't part of their core competencies. Upskilling is the process of gaining new and relevant skills that are needed now and in the future. Upskilling is critical in every industry. Following major shifts and pivots in workplaces around the world, it has become clear that not only do industries need to be adaptive, but their employees also need to be well-trained to deal with shifting expectations. Digital skills, analytics skills, and organizational transformation skills are all part of the upskilling initiative. Upskilling is crucial since it prepares employees for success in the workplace. Every employee will have distinct holes to fill when it comes to upskilling. In the virtual workplace, conducting a skills gap analysis to discover what each team member can improve on and combining them with career goals when planning is great. Virtual work models empower members of the Pods to be swapped out to bring in the relevant talents to complete the task at hand. A lack of abilities in a range of areas is referred to as the skills gap. These talents include everything from technical STEM skills to soft skills. As organizations continue to operate remotely and through digital channels, digital upskilling is more important than ever.

Sponsorship: Companies frequently sponsor events, trade exhibits, groups, or charitable causes in order to achieve certain commercial objectives and gain a competitive edge. Sponsorship is a type of marketing that helps to develop brand loyalty and persona. Educational programs, press releases, awards, banners, badge holders, audio-visual equipment, display PCs, shuttle buses, print on demand, podcasts, trade exhibitions, or other branded swag are all examples of sponsorships. Sponsoring events that are important to your clients generate positive thoughts about your company. Corporate sponsorship is a type of marketing in which a business pays to be connected with a project or activity. Sponsorship marketing is a marketing approach that is underutilized. The first and most obvious benefit of sponsorship marketing is the increased visibility of your business among potential clients. Backlinks have long been considered the holy grail of SEO marketing. One of the most underappreciated advantages of sponsorship is the ability to obtain a backlink. The sponsors of most organizations and events are listed on their website.

Ecommerce: Building a successful eCommerce firm requires intuition, market knowledge, a sound business plan, and thorough product and business model research. Due to the widespread and widespread adoption of online purchasing, eCommerce business models are now referred to as best sellers. E-commerce marketplaces are online marketplaces that connect buyers and merchants. They are adaptable and cost-effective, as they just require a little amount of setup time. Choosing and implementing the proper eCommerce business model for your online company may prove to be more difficult than you anticipated. Especially if you're a newcomer to the field. Knowing which model best fits your target niche, resources, and competencies is the first step toward success. The beauty of online commerce is that it allows you to sell almost anything. However, starting with a limited product line is always an excellent idea. Physical things, digital products, and services can all be sold in your store.

Influencer marketing: Social media has become an important aspect of people's lives, as well as a vital means for firms to reach new audiences. One of the most common blunders made by traditional media is failing to distinguish between celebrities and online influencers. It was tough to find a reputable vendor who could create and implement high-quality advertising prior to the social media boom. Influencer marketing is based on the use of social media influencers, many of whom would never consider themselves famous in a traditional sense. Influencer marketing incorporates the concept of celebrity endorsement into a content-driven marketing campaign. In the case of influencer marketing, the primary differentiation is that the campaign's results are collaborations between businesses and influencers.

Subscription: The huge success of ride-sharing, home-sharing, and office-sharing services demonstrate that there is an increasing need for services. A consumer pays a recurring payment in exchange for the usage of a product or service in the subscription business model. Subscription-based models are ideal for two types of businesses: those that provide content access and those that provide a repeat service. The subscription business model isn't going away anytime soon. Of course, subscriptions are one of the most common business models for modern software, but you'd be hard-pressed to find an industry that hasn't had at least one subscription success story in recent years. When done correctly, this method is a great instrument for growth. The subscription-based business model is gaining popularity. Previously dominated by newspapers, periodicals, gyms, utilities, and telecommunications companies, subscriptions now offer more products and services to more individuals than ever before.

www.ingramcontent.com/pod-product-compliance
Lightning Source LLC
Chambersburg PA
CBHW070905220526
45466CB00005B/2136